Contents

To my children, Serena and John, who have just tasted scuba diving for the first time.

1

Introduction

Acknowledgements
Text by Dave Saunders.
Special thanks to Michael Portelly, Mike Holbrook, Chris Hudd, Twickers World and Hilton International.
All photographs by Dave Saunders, except the following: Linda Pitkin: pp. 9 (top), 45, 47, inside back cover; Paul Springett: p. 46; Mark Webster: pp. 38, 39; F. Jack Jackson: p. 1; Mike Busuttili: pp. 18, 31; John Bantin: pp. 7, 8, 9 (bottom), 11 (bottom left), 12; A. P. Valves (Buddy): front cover, pp. 10 (left), 11 (top left), 20 (left), 35, back cover (right); Michael Portelly: inside front cover, pp. 17, 34, 41, 42, 44, back cover (left); Nikon: pp. 36, 43; Greenaway Marine (International) Ltd: p. 37.
Illustrations by 1-11 line-art.

Note Throughout the book divers are referred to individually as 'he'. This should, of course, be taken to mean 'he or she' where appropriate.

Also by Dave Saunders: *The Complete Scuba Diving Guide* (A & C Black).

Scuba diving is unlike anything else you will ever experience. Anticipation, excitement, wonder and exhilaration all combine to make diving uniquely rewarding. Ever since 1943, when Jacques Cousteau and Emile Gagnan produced the aqualung or Self-Contained Underwater Breathing Apparatus (SCUBA), sport diving has become more and more accessible to non-professional enthusiasts.

Scuba diving is one of the fastest growing sports, with millions of participants world-wide. Anyone above a minimum age (usually 16) who can swim and is reasonably fit and healthy can learn to dive. Today's sophisticated, comfortable and reliable equipment makes it easier and safer than ever to enjoy the underwater world first hand.

On holiday you can have a closely supervised 'taster' dive after only 10 minutes of instruction. However, if you want to take things further you should enroll on a reputable training scheme recognised by one of the sport's major training organisations (such as PADI, BSAC or SAA). You can join a club and progress through a series of lectures and training sessions, meeting once or twice a week; you can cover all the basic training on a full-time week's course at a specialised dive centre; or you can go on a diving holiday which incorporates all the necessary training. This book is intended to complement, rather than to replace, a recognised training course.

Scuba diving *is* a risk sport, and this adds to its appeal. Yet the risks are minimised through comprehensive training, good diving practices and regular servicing of equipment. Your diving qualification is your passport to explore rivers, lakes and the fringes of the oceans down to 40 m beneath the waves. Your equipment and knowledge enable you to get there and back safely.

Snorkelling

Equipment

In order to function effectively in and under the water, human beings need several props. When you begin diving you can hire or borrow what you need from a club or dive school. Before spending a lot of money on all the gear, establish that you definitely want to pursue the sport, then start selecting equipment to suit your needs. The following items of equipment are essential for snorkelling.

Mask and snorkel

A mask and snorkel enable you to swim on the surface without needing to lift your head in order to breathe.

The mask keeps the water out of your eyes so you can see clearly underwater. It should have a soft nose-pocket so you can pinch your nose when needing to clear your ears and breathe into the mask through your nose (*see* page 24). The mask has a waterproof seal and should fit the face snugly so that no water can trickle in through gaps. Test the mask on the surface by placing it on your face without using the straps. Then, by breathing in gently through your nose, you will create a small vacuum which holds the mask in position. If you wear glasses you can snap off the arms of an old pair and tape the specs inside your mask. Alternatively, prescription-lensed masks can be bought.

▼ *A mask enables you to see clearly underwater*

A snorkel is a 'J'-shaped, heavy-duty rubber tube, 43–5 cm long and just over 1 cm in diameter, with a mouthpiece at one end. This is inserted in the mouth and the two rubber lugs are gripped *gently* between the teeth. Bright orange tape around the top of the snorkel makes it clearly visible in the water. The snorkel can be attached to the mask strap by a loop or slipped between the strap and the diver's head. The snorkel should be retained when scuba diving and used on the surface when the diver wants to conserve his air supply.

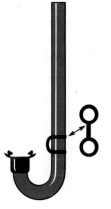

◀ *Fig. 1 By breathing through a snorkel you do not have to keep raising your head out of the water*

Fins

Fins provide a powerful thrust which can help you to tread water effortlessly or to propel yourself through the water smoothly and gracefully. In this way you seldom need to use your arms except for manoeuvring. Some fins have an adjustable heel strap; others have a pocket for the foot to slot into. Larger models often have vents to direct the flow of water through the fins on the up-kick, thus reducing resistence and increasing efficiency.

Technique

Snorkelling is a cheap and easy way to experience the underwater world. Confident use of mask, snorkel and fins enables you to explore the top 5 m of water, where you'll find much of the interesting life and colour.

First, rinse the fins so they are easier to slip on, then put them on. In order to prevent the mask misting up in the water, spit on the inside of the face-plate, wipe the saliva around and rinse it out. Clear any hair away from your face, hold the mask in position with one hand and pull the strap back over your head with the other. If the snorkel is not on a retaining loop, slip it under the mask strap just in front of your ear. Close your mouth around the mouth-piece, gently gripping it with your teeth.

◀ *Fig. 2 Some fins have a pouch for the foot; others have a heel strap*

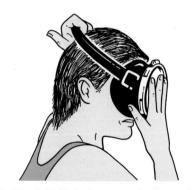

▲ *Fig. 3 Hold the hair away from your face and place the mask in position, then pull the strap over your head*

4

Breathing through your mouth, not your nose, place your head face down in the water. Keeping the end of the snorkel tube out of the water, float on the surface and get used to breathing. It requires a little more effort than usual because of the extra air in the tube that is taken in and out with each breath. If water splashes into the snorkel, or you need to clear the tube on surfacing after a duck dive, blow sharply into the mouthpiece.

Fins are like big webbed feet. They enable you to move quickly through the water with little effort. Treading water is also easier, and a broad 'scissors' movement of your legs keeps your head well above the surface. Good finning technique ensures that you move through the water with the minimum of effort. With hands at your sides or behind your back, and toes pointed, keep your legs straight (though not rigid). Then move your legs firmly up and down. This is a calm, controlled movement from the hips, and it should not involve a lot of splashing.

Fig. 5 Sequence of positions for a surface, ▶
or duck, dive

▲ *Fig. 4 Finning movement should be from the hips, with minimum bending at the knees*

To duck-dive and explore the underwater world at close quarters, begin by floating face down on the surface with your arms by your side. Take a medium-sized breath, then bend at the waist so your head and torso are submerged. The weight of your legs as you bring them straight up out of the water will push you down. A single powerful arm stroke will take you deep enough to begin finning underwater. When you return to the surface look up and hold one arm above your head to avoid hitting anything. On the surface tip your head forwards and blow the water out of the snorkel with a short, sharp breath.

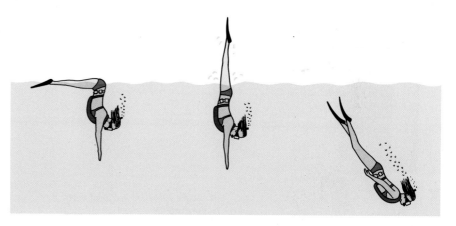

Scuba diving

Equipment

As human beings are not equipped to extract oxygen from water, we need to take our own air supply when staying beneath the surface for any length of time.

◀ *Scuba cylinders are filled with compressed air*

Aqualung

The aqualung enables the diver to breathe normally at depth. It comprises a *harness* which is worn like a rucksack, a *cylinder* of compressed air, and a *regulator*.

Cylinders come in a range of sizes – from 6 to 15 litres – and are marked with such information as the capacity (size), the date of manufacture, and the date of the last test. They are made of either steel or aluminium, the latter type being lighter, bigger and rust-free. At the top of the cylinder is the *cylinder valve* with a tap to open or shut off the air supply. A full cylinder contains air which is under considerable pressure. The cylinder must be internally inspected every year to check for corrosion or other damage.

The regulator controls the flow of air from the cylinder, enabling the diver to breathe at the correct pressure underwater. It comprises a flexible rubber hose with a valve at either end to reduce the air pressure to a breathable level. The first valve, or *stage*, is attached to the cylinder valve on the cylinder by means of an 'A' clamp. This reduces the pressure of the air in the cylinder to a constant level above ambient pressure.

The demand valve, or second stage, further reduces the air pressure to that of the surrounding water. This section includes the mouthpiece which is gripped gently between the teeth; a purge button which releases a continuous flow of air; and exhaust vents for expelled air. When the diver breathes in through the mouthpiece, the suction moves a flexible diaphragm attached to a lever which opens a valve to release air from the tube, making it available 'on demand'. When he breathes out, the diaphragm returns to its original position, stopping the flow of air.

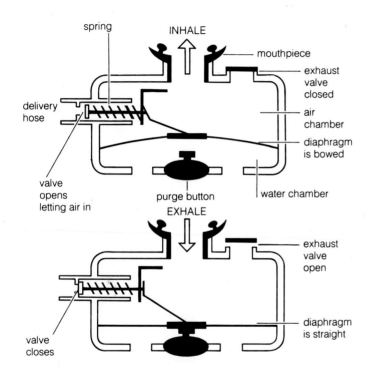

spring

INHALE

mouthpiece

delivery hose

exhaust valve closed

air chamber

diaphragm is bowed

valve opens letting air in

purge button

water chamber

EXHALE

exhaust valve open

diaphragm is straight

valve closes

▲ *Fig. 6 The second stage of the regulator, or mouthpiece, reduces the pressure of the air in the cylinder to the correct pressure for breathing*

Most training schemes now recommend the use of an *octopus rig*. This is a spare second stage. If one demand valve develops a fault the diver can switch to using the other, or if your buddy runs out of air he can readily share your supply without you needing to remove your own mouthpiece.

To enable the diver to monitor the pressure of air left in the cylinder, a pressure gauge is attached to the first stage by a hose. The first stage may have other medium-pressure ports to supply air to a lifejacket or dry suit.

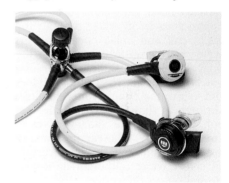

▲ *An octopus rig is a spare second stage which can be used if your buddy runs out of air or if your mouthpiece develops a fault*

Diving suit

A diving suit helps you to retain body warmth and avoid scratches and bruises. There are two main types of diving suit: the wet suit and the dry suit. There is also the semi-dry suit which is basically a more efficient type of wet suit.

Wet suits are made of neoprene foam sandwiched between nylon linings. Modern designs are often colourful and stylish. They are available as a one-piece suit, as trousers and jacket, or as dungaree and jacket, and usually have separate hood, gloves and bootees.

Wet suits let in water through the neck, cuff and ankle openings. This water warms up in contact with the body, forming an insulating layer. The suit should be closely fitting so it does not allow too much water to flush through. A thin (3 mm), 'shortie' wet suit is adequate for shallow dives in tropical waters, whereas neoprene of 6 mm or 7 mm keeps the diver warmer in colder water (although he forfeits flexibility).

Neoprene **semi-dry suits** have the cuff and ankle seals of a dry suit but the

▲ Left *The neoprene wet suit traps a layer of water next to your body which warms up and provides insulation.* Right *The membrane dry suit has cuff and neck seals to keep your body dry*

design of a wet suit. They let water in at the neck, but it does not flush through.

As **dry suits** keep divers essentially dry, they are popular in cold climates. The suit is often one-piece, though the hood and bootees are sometimes separate.

There are two types of dry suit: *neoprene* and *membrane*. A neoprene dry suit is usually entered through an opening in the upper back, which is then sealed with a sturdy waterproof zip. Compressed neoprene suits are less bulky, less buoyant, more flexible and more durable.

A membrane dry suit is made of thinner, lighter-weight material. It is loose-fitting and worn with clothing underneath, such as a purpose-made 'woolly bear' suit.

The amount of air in dry suits can be controlled. Generally, a direct feed line from the first stage of the regulator supplies air to the upper chest of the suit. An exhaust or *dump valve* can be opened to vent excess air. As more air is trapped within a dry suit than in a wet suit, the diver is kept warmer, but more weights are needed to keep him submerged.

Weight belt

Divers need to carry extra weight in order to compensate for the buoyancy of their wet or dry suits. Lead weights are generally worn in a weight belt around the waist. The amount of weight needed varies according to the physiological make-up of the diver, the type of suit he is wearing and whether he is diving in salt or fresh water. A diver is more buoyant in salt water and therefore needs about 2 kg more weight. As the weight belt may need to be jettisoned in an emergency, it must have a quick-release buckle which can be operated easily even when the diver is wearing gloves.

◄ *A weight belt enables the diver to remain below the surface despite the buoyancy of his diving suit*

9

Lifejacket

A lifejacket is an essential item of equipment and no dive should be attempted without one. It allows a diver to adjust buoyancy at depth, it can help bring him to the surface, and it provides support at the surface.

▲ *Today's sophisticated lifejackets have many safety features, including an emergency air cylinder, a choice of breathing valves, dump valves and quick release buckles*

Buoyancy aids and surface lifejackets are *not* suitable for divers, but may be used by boat handlers or by snorkellers.

A 'Stab' or Stabilizer jacket usually has an integral backpack to house the main cylinder. It is worn like a waistcoat, and is comfortable and easy to put on. An adjustable buoyancy lifejacket (ABLJ) fits over the head and is worn like a bib. Unlike the Stab jacket it is not attached to the main cylinder.

Most jackets can be inflated via a direct feed line from the regulator first stage. This is operated by pressing a button. Some have a small cylinder of compressed air independent of the main cylinder. This is operated by turning a tap on the small cylinder. Lifejackets can also be inflated orally, but this requires care and co-ordination and is not recommended for stressful situations.

Air can be vented from one or more dump valves in the top of the jacket.

▲ *A dive watch should be easy to read and have a rotating bezel which can be set to the dive start time*

Dive watch

A diver must constantly monitor his depth and the length of time he is underwater. A waterproof dive watch with a luminous face can be read even in murky water. A rotating bezel around the face can be set to the position of the minute hand at the beginning of the dive.

Depth gauge

A depth gauge enables the diver to monitor his depth, thus helping him to avoid potential problems associated with deep diving (*see* pp. 32–3). The depth gauge should indicate the maximum, as well as the current, depth reached during a dive. It can be worn on the wrist or can be a part of a console of instruments.

▲ *A four-gauge console with a thermometer, pressure gauge, depth gauge and compass*

▼ *Dive computers are useful aids, but should not replace good diving practice*

Dive computer

Although a diver should understand and adhere to the dive tables, a dive computer can act as a safeguard and can provide a lot of additional information. The computer is activated automatically when immersed in water. It constantly monitors changes in pressure and adjusts dive times, decompression stops, ascent rate and surface interval times. An alarm sounds if you stray outside safe limits.

Other dive accessories

A diver also needs a *knife* to free himself or his buddy from a rope or net; a *compass* for underwater navigation; a *torch* to explore nooks and crannies, to bring out true colours and for night dives; a *dive bag* to hold his gear; a small *medical kit*; and a *log book* to record dives. A *surface marker buoy* (SMB), attached by a line to a reel held by a diver, gives those on the surface an indication of his location. The *divers' flag* is the International Code Flag 'A' – white and blue. Mounted on a boat or SMB, it warns those nearby that divers are down.

▲ *A dive knife is kept in a sheath strapped to a leg or arm*

11

▲ *A dive torch restores natural colours and is essential on night dives*

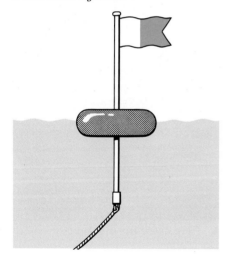

◄ *Fig. 7 A surface marker buoy with the 'Divers down' flag is attached by a line to the divers beneath the surface*

Care of equipment

Looking after dive gear not only prolongs its life but also helps avoid malfunctions. Frequent servicing is especially important for regulators, cylinders and lifejackets. After each day's diving, all equipment should be rinsed in fresh water to minimise corrosion from salt water or deterioration of rubber caused by chlorine in swimming pools. An application of light oil on all zips helps to keep them rust-free.

Membership of a diving organisation may include third party liability insurace cover. Equipment should also be covered for loss or damage.

The effects of water

Pressure

A diver underwater is subject to pressure from all sides due to the weight of water above him. The change in pressure is most pronounced near the surface. The normal atmospheric pressure at the surface is approximately equal to 1 bar. At 10 m down, the pressure is increased to 2 bar, i.e. twice the surface pressure. At 20 m the pressure is 3 bar. At 30 m the pressure is 4 bar.

Water pressure has a marked affect on any air that goes down with the diver and his equipment. As the water pressure increases with depth, the air, other than that in the cylinder, is compressed into a smaller volume. At 10 m below the surface the volume of air is half that at the surface. Conversely, on ascent the pressure decreases and the air expands. As a result you must breathe out as you ascend to avoid damaging your lungs. This is *not* a problem when snorkelling and duck-diving as the air breathed in at the surface is not compressed air.

depth	pressure
sea level	1 bar
10 m	2 bar
20 m	3 bar
30 m	4 bar

Buoyancy

The gas (nitrogen) in a wet suit, and the air in a dry suit and lifejacket, is compressed on descent and expands on ascent. Thus your total volume decreases as you descend and you become less buoyant. If you are neutrally buoyant at the surface – i.e. you don't go up or down – you will be negatively buoyant at 20 m or 30 m and need to compensate by inflating the lifejacket or dry suit. In contrast, as you ascend the air expands, your total volume increases and you become more buoyant. As this will speed up your ascent rate, you will need to vent air from the lifejacket.

◄ *Fig. 8 The deeper you go, the greater the pressure. At 10 m down, air is compressed to half its volume. At 20 m it is reduced to a third, and at 30 m to a quarter of its original volume*

Clearing ears

The increase in pressure also affects the air cavities in the ears. As you descend, the water pressure increases. This pushes the ear drum from the outside and can cause pain followed by a burst ear drum if the pressure either side is not equalised. This can be done by swallowing, or by holding your nose and gently trying to blow through it. These actions open the eustachian tube and allow air from the lungs to enter the middle ear, equalising the pressure either side of the ear drum. Don't dive when you have a cold or ear/sinus infection, and don't use ear plugs.

Mask squeeze

As pressure increases during descent, the volume of air in the mask decreases and the mask 'squeezes' on to the face. You can easily equalise the pressure by breathing out through your nose into the mask.

Air consumption

To enable the lungs to expand normally at depth, air must be supplied at the same pressure as the surrounding water. A mechanism within the regulator does just that, compressing the air that you breathe as you descend. As a result you consume air more quickly at depth – at 10 m you breathe twice as much air as at the surface, at 20 m three times as much, and at 30 m four times as much.

Air is also consumed more quickly when the diver is cold, tense, unfit or particularly energetic.

Nitrogen narcosis

At depths greater than 30 m the concentration of nitrogen within the compressed air breathed by the diver can cause nitrogen narcosis or 'the narcs'. The symptoms include a feeling of light-headedness, disorientation and loss of reason. The effects of nitrogen narcosis can be reversed simply by ascending.

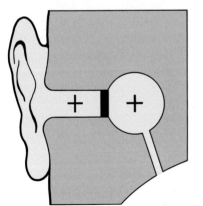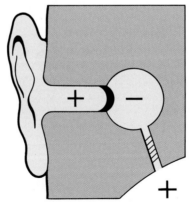

▲ *Fig. 9 As pressure increases with depth, the ear drum is pushed in. To equalise pressure either side of the drum, swallow or hold the nose, close the mouth and try to force air out*

14

Decompression sickness or 'the bends'

When under pressure the lungs absorb nitrogen as well as oxygen. Some of the nitrogen dissolves into the bloodstream and body tissues. The longer a diver stays down, and the deeper he goes, the more nitrogen enters his system. As he surfaces, the ambient pressure is reduced and the nitrogen returns to the lungs and is dissipated. If he ascends too rapidly the nitrogen bubbles will not have time to dissipate and will be caught in the blood vessels and body tissues. The trapped bubbles will expand as the diver continues to ascend and can block the blood circulation or damage the nervous system.

Symptoms of 'the bends' include pain in the joints and muscles, paralysis, and sometimes loss of consciousness. As the effects are not always immediately apparent a diver with suspected decompression sickness should be closely observed for up to 24 hours after the dive. If symptoms develop, the diver should be put into a *recompression chamber*. This is a chamber in which the pressure can be increased to that of

the deepest point of the dive. The nitrogen bubbles should then recompress so that they disappear. The pressure can be decreased slowly so the bubbles dissipate and do not re-form.

▲ *In a recompression chamber a diver can be recompressed to the pressure he reached while diving. Then he can be decompressed in a controlled manner*

15

Decompression sickness can be avoided by diving within the safety limits outlined in the dive tables (*see* pp. 32–3). Deep dives may require 'decompression stops' during ascent, to give the nitrogen time to escape. Accurate buoyancy control is the key to successful decompression stops.

Burst lung

As you ascend, the ambient pressure decreases and the air in the lungs expands. If the diver does not breathe out, this can rupture the lung lining and air can enter either the bloodstream or the tissues around the lungs. The diver will feel dizzy, numb or become paralysed; he will have difficulty breathing and may become unconscious. A damaged lung can be avoided by not holding your breath, but breathing normally on ascent. It is treated by recompressing the diver.

Hypothermia

Water is a good conductor of heat and can quickly conduct heat away from the body. In water cooler than 20°C a diving suit is needed to avoid the speedy onset of hypothermia. If hypothermia is detected, the first priority is to restore warmth to the body. If possible make sure the person is in a warm sheltered place, remove the wet suit, then dry and dress him quickly. If he is wearing a dry suit, wrap him in a blanket or put him in a survival bag. Keep him calm and still. Give him a warm drink, but nothing alcoholic.

Colour absorption

The colours of the spectrum are progressively filtered out as they pass through water. Red light is absorbed first, so that at about 5 m from the surface, reds appear black. Then orange, yellow and green are filtered out, until at about 25 m everything seems to be black or grey. Artificial light, from a torch or video lamp, is needed to bring out the true colours of the marine environment.

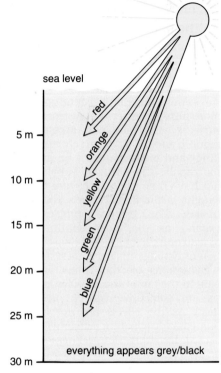

▲ *Fig. 10 Colours from the sun are progressively absorbed or filtered out by the water*

Light refraction

When light passes from water into the air-space trapped in your face mask, it is refracted or 'bent'. This makes underwater objects seem one-third bigger than they really are, and only three-quarters of their actual distance away.

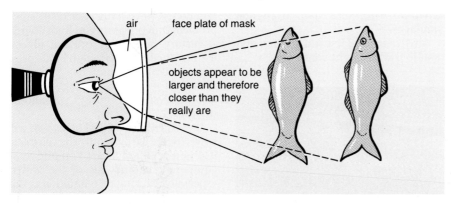

▲ *Fig. 11 Light rays passing from water to air are bent or 'refracted'*

Sound transmission

The underwater world is far from silent. Besides your own breathing, you can hear waves breaking on rocks or disturbing shingle, a diver tapping on his cylinder with the butt-end of a knife, and even the sound of a fish crunching coral in its jaws. Sound is transmitted faster in water than on land; sea mammals such as whales make good use of this by communicating across thousands of miles.

Natural hazards

Most sea creatures keep a safe distance away from divers, but you need to be aware of the few that could cause harm. In tropical waters the beautiful lion fish has poisonous dorsal spines. Stone fish, scorpion fish and certain jelly fish can inflict an excruciatingly painful, even fatal, wound. The barbed spines of sea urchins are difficult to remove and can become infected. Other marine life to avoid includes fire coral, so-called because of the burning rash it produces. Stings and burns should be treated with alcohol, antihistamine, lemon juice or vinegar.

Lion fish have poisonous spines on their dorsal fins ▶

First Aid

Each diver should have his own small medical kit containing the following: adhesive dressings, cotton wool, crepe bandage, triangular bandage, butterfly stitches, safety pins, scissors, tweezers, antiseptic cream, lip and sun cream, aspirin, eye drops.

A group of divers should have easy access to a larger medical kit containing all the above, plus: a thermometer, a survival bag, a range of sterile dressings, a roll of zinc oxide plaster (25 mm × 5 m), and four triangular bandages.

Always take a First Aid kit on a dive boat in a water-tight container.

▲ *Underwater manoeuvres are usually slow and relaxed*

Fit to dive

Before you begin diving in open water you will need to have a medical check-up and chest X-ray to make sure that you do not have a heart or respiratory problem that prevents you from diving. A history of epilepsy, mental illness, asthma, heart disease, high blood pressure or diabetes may bar you from diving. If you have a cold and are unable to clear your ears you should not dive.

If you are fairly fit and agile, you will cope more easily with the physical exertion required to get you and your equipment in and out of the water, especially in choppy conditions. But sport diving does not normally call for great strength or stamina. Scuba gear which is heavy and cumbersome on the surface becomes apparently weightless under the water, and manoeuvring underwater is usually easy and relaxing.

A few simple stretching and warming-up exercises before a dive will increase the circulation and help keep you supple and alert during the dive.

Using scuba gear

SCUBA (Self-Contained Underwater Breathing Apparatus) enables you to continue breathing while underwater. Learn to use the equipment from a qualified instructor. This is safer, more fun and a great confidence builder. Never dive alone. Stay close to your buddy at all times, as assistance will be required quickly in the event of an incident.

Be methodical in the preparation of your equipment, and check the functioning of all the gear while you are on the surface, where it is much easier to sort out any problems.

Remove the dust cap from the cylinder valve on the top of the cylinder, which has been filled with compressed air. Place the first stage of the regulator over the valve and screw it on hand-tight. Turn on the air supply tap and the various hoses will immediately fill with air. Look at the pressure gauge to check the air pressure in the cylinder. Check the regulator works properly by breathing through the mouthpiece. Then turn off the air until you are ready to enter the water.

◀ *The first stage of the regulator is screwed on to the valve on the top of the main cylinder. The air is then turned on using the on-off tap*

▲ *The pressue guage is checked to make sure there is plenty of air for the dive*

19

If the lifejacket is separate from the cylinder put it on first, followed by the aqualung then the weight belt. At the end of a dive the weight belt and aqualung may be removed and handed to someone in the boat or on a jetty, while the diver retains his lifejacket at all times in the water. Many lifejackets incorporate the pouch or band which holds the main cylinder, in which case both are put on together, before the weight belt.

Put your arms through the straps and lift the aqalung on to your back like a backpack. Tighten the straps if necessary to minimise movement of the cylinder. Then fasten the quick-release buckle on the waist strap.

◀ *The weight belt must be put on after the lifejacket in case you need to jettison the weight belt in an emergency*

Carry out a buddy ▶ check to ensure that you know how to release each other's weight belts and operate each other's lifejackets

Buddy diving

Never dive alone. Always dive with a partner, or buddy, and keep an eye on each other. If one of you gets into difficulty underwater the other must be close at hand to help. When you are kitting up, check each other's gear. Help each other put on your cylinders. Make sure you can locate and operate your buddy's weight belt buckle and can inflate his lifejacket.

Hand signals

Although underwater voice communication systems are available, all divers must learn to communicate by sign language. Before entering the water, go through with your buddy the basic hand signals needed when communicating underwater.

The *OK* signal, which is used repeatedly, is a clear 'O' made using the thumb and forefinger, while keeping the other three fingers straight and together. This means, 'Are you OK?' and should always be followed by the same signal in response ('Yes I am OK.'). On the surface the same signal is used, but with the arm extended.

Something is wrong or *Not OK* is a flat hand, palm down, rocked from side to side. Something needs to be done before you continue. This may be simply pausing a moment while your buddy clears his ears or adjusts his buoyancy.

Help! is a more urgent signal requiring immediate attention. It is made by waving a clenched fist from side to side.

Under the water the elbow is kept bent; on the surface the arm is stretched out.

Going down or *Let's go down* is a thumbs-down signal often used at the beginning of a dive.

Going up or *Let's go up* is a thumbs-up sign, which may be used to mark the end of a dive.

I'm out of breath is shown by moving your hands backwards and forwards against the lower chest, indicating rapid breathing. Both of you should stop and allow time to recover.

I'm short of air is a clenched fist held still, with fingers facing your buddy. This is followed by *Let's go up*.

I have no more air is a chopping movement made with the flat of the hand against the throat. Constant monitoring of your air pressure should prevent this situation from ever arising, but if it does, your buddy should immediately offer his own mouthpiece or spare second stage of his octopus rig in order to share his air supply.

▲ Fig. 12 Hand signals
Stop, stay where you are

▲ **Go up** *or* **I'm going up**

▲ **I'm OK** *or* **Are you OK?**
(This can be a question or a response.)

21

▲ **You** or **Me** or **Let's swim in this direction**

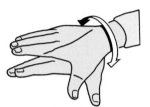

▲ **Something is wrong** or **Not OK**
(The hand is rocked from side to side.)

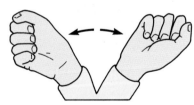

▲ **Help!** *(The distress signal is made by waving the clenched fist. Underwater the arm is bent; on the surface the arm is stretched out.)*

▲ **I have no more air**
(A chopping movement to the neck.)

▲ **I am out of breath** *(Hands move forwards and backwards to the lower chest.)*

▲ *During a buddy check, make sure you agree on the basic signals*

Entering the water

In a swimming pool, first check that the water is deep enough, then insert the mouthpiece. Hold the mask against your face with one hand and support the cylinder on your back with the other. Now enter in one of four ways:

- take a long stride
- slide in from a sitting position
- do a forward roll
- do a backward roll.

Fig. 13 The four most common ways of ▶ entering the water in full kit: by taking a long stride, slipping in from a sitting position, using a forward roll or backward roll

Mask clearing

Even if your mask fits perfectly it may be knocked and let in water, so you need to know how to clear it. On the surface this can be done easily by simply lifting the bottom of the mask so the water drains away.

When clearing the mask underwater, tip your head back, press the top of the mask with the fingers of one hand and breathe out through your nose. The additional air being blown into the mask will escape along the edge which offers the least resistance. As you are holding the top of the mask, the air will escape along the bottom, forcing the water out first.

▲ *Fig. 14 Hold the strap in one hand and the mask in the other. Place the mask over the eyes and pull the strap behind your head. Dispel the water by pressing the top of the mask, tilting your head back and breathing out through your nose*

Fig. 15 In a spread-eagle position, test ▶ *your buoyancy. When you are neutrally buoyant you should ascend slowly after breathing in, and descend after breathing out*

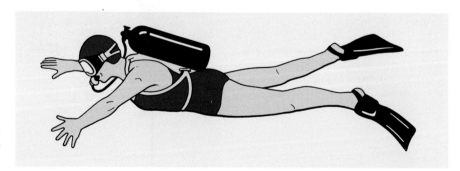

Buoyancy control

If you are not wearing a wet suit, only a small amount of weight – perhaps 2 kg – is needed to keep you submerged. A diver is much more buoyant with a full wet suit and when in salt water.

To test your buoyancy, position yourself face down, spread-eagled at the bottom of the pool or in 2–4 m of water. Take a deep breath and hold it. The additional air in your lungs will increase your buoyancy. If you remain on the bottom, you are *negatively buoyant*. Increase your buoyancy by inflating the lifejacket slightly or removing some weight. When you fill your lungs with air this time, you should start to float up. Breathe out again and you will sink to the bottom. You are now *neutrally buoyant* and do not have to work hard to keep yourself down (if you are positively buoyant) or to prevent yourself from sinking (if you are negatively buoyant).

Fig. 16 Relative buoyancy without a wet ▶
suit, with a wet suit, and with a wet suit and weight belt

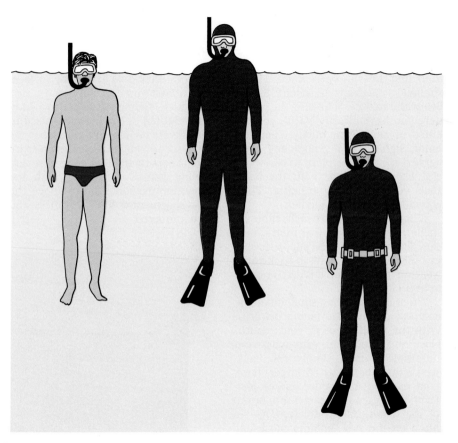

Open water diving

Your first dives in open water will be shallow – perhaps to about 8–9 m below the surface. Following the procedure you have already learnt, you get kitted up with your buddy, checking hand signals and equipment. You agree a simple dive plan: to carry out and become familiar with the basic skills covered during training. Then you enter the water together.

When diving from a beach, choose a sheltered entry point free from obstacles. Either walk in, then put on the fins in 1 m of water; or walk in backwards wearing the fins until it is deep enough to begin finning.

When diving from a small inflatable boat, sit on the side facing inwards. With the mouthpiece in your mouth, place one hand over your mask and mouthpiece, then simply roll backwards into the water. A larger 'hard' boat may have a ladder and/or platform, making it easy to get into or out of the water. Alternatively, you can jump off the side, holding mask and cylinder (if the side is not too high above the water).

After exchanging *OK* signals with your buddy and with the surface cover, you both duck-dive below the surface. From a boat you descend down a *shot line*, which is a line – attached to a buoy and weighted at the bottom – used to guide divers on descent and ascent. As you descend you equalise the pressure in your ears by holding your nose and blowing gently. Compared with the heavy, cumbersome figure above the surface, you now feel weightless and unencumbered.

At the bottom exchange *OK* signals again, then check your pressure gauge. If you are negatively buoyant, i.e. you tend to sink, then inflate the lifejacket slightly using the direct feed from the main cylinder or by turning the tap on the small cylinder of compressed air.

At the beginning of a dive it is a good idea to fin into the current. Thus, during the second half of the dive when you may be tired you are finning with the current. Once back at the shot line at the end of the dive your buddy gives the thumbs up signal for *Going up*.

▲ *Give the OK signal to someone in the boat before you dive and when you surface at the end of a dive*

◄ *The easiest way to enter the water from an inflatable boat is to roll over backwards*

Ascent procedure

You should return to the surface in a slow and controlled manner. Gently fin towards the surface, keeping an eye on each other and looking up while rotating to watch for obstacles. Do not hold your breath as you ascend; remember, the air in your lungs expands as the pressure decreases, and failing to breathe out may result in damaged lungs. Also, any air in the buoyancy aid will expand on ascent and should be vented to prevent you from accelerating towards the surface.

Make sure you go up slowly; at about 15 m per minute, or no faster than your smallest, slowest bubbles. If you are using a surface marker buoy, wind up the line. As you near the surface look up and hold one arm above your head to protect it from unseen obstacles. On the surface check for nearby hazards, partially inflate your lifejacket, and exchange the *OK* signal with your buddy and with someone in the boat or on the shore. Most diving accidents happen at the surface, so continue using your regulator until you leave the water.

▲ *Fig. 17 Look up and all around as you ascend. Raise one arm as you near the surface as protection against unexpected objects*

Air sharing

An octopus rig is a spare second stage which enables two divers to breathe from a single cylinder of air. Although octopus rigs are now quite common, you need to learn how to share a single regulator in case you or your buddy do not have an octopus rig.

As long as you constantly check your air supply, and begin the ascent with the cylinder at least a quarter full, you should never have to share air. But if you do run out of air or your regulator malfunctions, air sharing, or buddy breathing, enables you to breathe air from your buddy's cylinder, and vice versa.

Hold on to each other's harness so you keep in close contact. When you signal that you require air – chopping action to the neck – your buddy (the donor) takes the initiative. Keeping hold of his own mouthpiece, he removes it and directs it towards your mouth. You help guide it into your mouth, pressing the purge button to blow the water away. After breathing in, out and in again, you let the donor have the mouthpiece back. In the meantime he has been slowly breathing out so he is immediately ready to take a fresh breath of air. Then the sequence is repeated.

Breathing out while you wait for the mouthpiece is also important because you would normally be ascending while sharing air and the air in your lungs would be expanding.

▲ *Fig. 18 When sharing air, hold on to your buddy's harness strap*

Lifesaving

Hopefully you will never have to carry out a real emergency rescue. By being aware of the dangers, following good diving procedure and maintaining equipment, most accidents can be avoided. The risk of accidents is greater on deep dives, in poor visibility and in a current. But your most vulnerable time is on the surface at the end of a dive. You may be tired, cold, short of air and it may be choppy.

In the event of an incident, the confidence you have built up during training will help you remain calm and in control of the situation. You must:

- assess the situation
- plan what to do
- act quickly.

Let's consider the most pessimistic scenario. If you can handle this basic procedure for rescuing an unconscious diver from depth you'll be a most reassuring buddy.

- Free the diver if he is trapped.
- Grip his harness.
- Inflate his lifejacket if you need more buoyancy.
- Press your clenched fist into his stomach to encourage him to breathe out during the ascent.
- Check your ascent rate – no faster than your slowest, smallest bubbles.
- Vent some air from the lifejacket if you are ascending too quickly.
- Check for obstacles near the surface.
- On the surface remove his mouthpiece and mask and check his airway is clear.
- If he is not breathing, apply mouth-to-nose resuscitation (which is easier to perform in the water than mouth-to-mouth). With the victim's head tilted back and supported with one hand, hold his mouth closed with your other hand on his chin and thumb over his mouth.
- Fin hard to raise yourself above his head while tilting his body towards you.
- Seal his nose with your mouth and blow air into his lungs.
- Give four quick breaths then establish a rhythm of one breath every four or five seconds.
- Inflate his lifejacket to about three-quarters full, and inflate your own lifejacket.
- Summon help by waving a clenched fist.
- Between breaths tow him towards the boat or shore if help is not immediately forthcoming. Use an extended arm tow, swimming on your back with your arm extended. If the casualty is conscious, grip the harness or lifejacket strap. If the casualty is unconscious, hold him under the chin with your hand in a pistol grip position and other hand under his neck. Stop every 20 seconds to apply four quick breaths.
- On the boat or shore, feel for a pulse on his neck (carotid artery). If his heart has stopped beating, carry out cardiac massage with the patient lying face up. With both hands together, palms down, position the bottom one just above the base of the sternum. Keeping your arms straight, press down sharply and release six times in quick succession.

- Establish whether or not he has started breathing. If not, continue resuscitation using mouth-to-mouth. With the head well back, pinch the nose with one hand and hold the mouth open by supporting the chin with the other.
- If there's no response, apply six more compressions of cardiac massage.
- Continue six compressions to one breath until you detect a pulse. Then continue resuscitation until breathing starts or medical help arrives.
- Once breathing, put him in the coma position with the head well back.

Carrying out a full rescue is physically and emotionally exhausting and should be carried out by two people where possible.

Always seek medical advice after an accident, even if the diver appears to have recovered fully.

▲ *Fig. 19 Lifesaving. Mouth-to-nose resuscitation in the water*

▲ *Summon help at the surface using the distress signal*

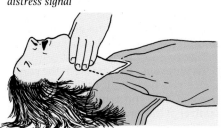

▲ *Check the carotid artery for a pulse*

Tow a conscious casualty by holding a ▶ strap. Tow an unconscious casualty by holding his chin with one hand and support his neck with the other

With the head well back, the coma ▶ position keeps the airway clear and does not restrict movement of the chest

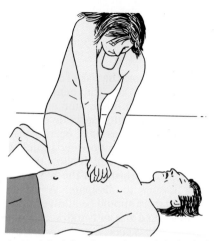

▲ With both hands together and the heel of the bottom hand just above the base of the sternum, press down with a firm movement

▲ On a boat or on land, use mouth-to-mouth resuscitation

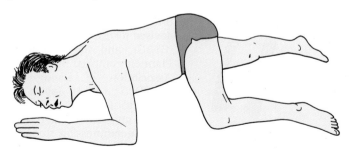

Emergency ascents

Sharing air while surfacing in a controlled manner is called an *assisted ascent*. A *free ascent* involves a single diver surfacing in a controlled manner, breathing out all the way. A *buoyant ascent* is faster because the diver's life-jacket is inflated in an emergency. It is a rapid ascent with the risk of a burst lung and/or the bends.

▲ *Fig. 20 Three types of emergency ascent:* from left to right – *assisted; free; buoyant*

Dive tables

In order to avoid the risk of decompression sickness, or 'the bends', dives deeper than 9 m have time and depth limits beyond which sport divers must not go. Dive tables have been devised by several organisations as a guide to safe diving limits, which allow time for nitrogen absorbed into the blood and body tissues to dissipate. A greater safety margin should be allowed when diving in cold and/or rough seas where the visibility is poor, than in clear tropical water. When planning a series of dives, each dive should be shallower than the last.

The tables most frequently used are the BSAC '88 Decompression Tables, devised for the British Sub-Aqua Club (BSAC), and the Recreational Dive Planner, compiled by the Professional Association of Diving Instructors (PADI). The BSAC tables include an option to decompress at the end of a dive to give the nitrogen time to dissipate. Decompression stops at 9m and 6m should only be planned by experienced divers. Sufficient air must be allowed to include time spent decompressing. The PADI tables are designed for dives which do *not* include a decompression stop. It is potentially dangerous to juggle tables compiled by different organisations in an attempt to increase the length of the dive.

Although dive computers constantly assess such factors as your depth, time and ascent rate, it is important to understand the dive tables and to plan and monitor a dive for yourself. Obtain a full set of tables before diving in open water. The tables here indicate only the *limits* of safe sport diving.

When calculating the duration of a dive, the deepest point of the dive must be used, even if you are there for a very short time.

Table 1 Maximum time allowed for a single dive without decompression stops (BSAC '88 Tables)

Depth (metres)	Minutes beyond which decompression stops are required
9	243
12	122
15	74
18	51
21	37
24	30
27	24
30	20
33	17
36	14
39	13
42	12
45	10
48	9
51	8

Table 2 Maximum time allowed for a single dive, beyond which a safety stop of 3 mins at 5 m is required (Recreational Dive Planner)

Depth (metres)	Minutes beyond which a safety stop is required	Limit of no-decompression dive
10	145	219
12	108	147
14	77	98
16	60	72
18	48	56
20	38	45
22	30	37
25	23	29
30	0	20
35	0	14
40	0	9
42	0	8

Extend your diving

As you become more involved in diving, you may decide to take advanced diving, instructor and lifesaving courses. Your basic qualification is just the beginning, a passport to a wide and varied diving world. With recognised certification you can hire equipment from dive centres around the world and explore different coastal waters, lakes and rivers.

Night dives offer a dramatic new dimension to the sport. As your sense of sight is considerably restricted, you need to be especially confident in your equipment, your buddy and your ability. Everyone on the dive must carry a torch, which should be turned on throughout the dive. Then, if one of the torches fails you can share with your buddy, and if a torch is dropped it can be easily located. A night dive should be shallow, and it is advisable to stay close to the point of entry. Watch the details of the marine life around you rather than trying to cover great distances.

▲ *A good torch is essential on a night dive*

A **drift dive** in a moderate current (4–6 knots) is an exhilarating experience. It requires good surface cover and careful planning. After entering the water from a boat you descend to an agreed depth, with one of the buddy pair holding the line to a surface marker buoy. As you are swept along by the current past reef walls or marine caves, the boat follows the buoy and should be ready to collect you at the end of the dive.

River dives can be rewarding in terms of what you see and what you find! Many divers explore river beds for old bottles, jars and assorted bric-a-brac. Others help boatmen retrieve lost anchors and ropes. Near urban centres, you must assess the potential hazards of dumped bicycles, beds and supermarket trolleys, as well as pollution. Be aware of the current and make sure you have a safe exit point if you are swept downstream.

Wreck dives have the romantic appeal of sunken treasure on Spanish galleons. In reality you usually find sections of non-descript metal, often heavily encrusted with marine life. All wrecks belong to someone and permission should be obtained from the owner before anything is salvaged. When venturing inside a wreck, wear a wet suit to protect you from scratches, take a torch and knife, and use a life line so you can find your way out. Constantly monitor your pressure gauge, depth gauge and dive time.

▲ *A disaster at sea becomes an adventure playground for divers*

Underwater photography and video

Whether you're shooting stills or video film, a record of your sport is inspiring, tangible evidence of what you have experienced. Before taking underwater filming seriously you must first be totally confident about diving. As photography can be time-consuming, you must agree with your buddy before the dive how much emphasis will be placed on picture-taking.

With the minimum of fuss, pictures can be taken through a glass-bottom bucket or glass-bottom boat, using a land camera. The closer and brighter the subject, the better the result.

The Nikonos RS single lens reflex ▶
underwater camera

Types of camera

Beneath the surface, stills and video images can be shot using an underwater camera, or a land camera in an underwater housing. There are several underwater point-and-shoot 35 mm compact cameras on the market. They are ideal for beginners and can take reasonable pictures when the subject is well lit and in clear water. The underwater camera used by most divers is the 35 mm single-lens reflex Nikonos. More recent models incorporate motordrive, interchangeable lenses including a zoom lens, several focusing modes including autofocus, and a choice of exposure controls including auto-exposure.

Alternatively, underwater housings are available for most land cameras – stills or video. These watertight containers have large operating knobs linked to focusing, aperture and trigger controls. As framing the picture is difficult when wearing a mask, a plastic frame can be attached to the top of some cameras.

▲ *Sony VXI video camera and Seapro underwater housing*

Problems with water

Sea water is bad news for land cameras and the inside of underwater cameras. Great care is needed in order to avoid soaking the electrics and to prevent corrosion.

Water also affects picture-taking. As light is refracted by water, objects appear closer than they really are. Thus a 35 mm lens on a 35 mm camera underwater is approximately equivalent to a 50 mm lens on land. In addition, suspended particles in the water reduce visibility and diffuse the light. The closer the camera is to the subject, the less suspended material there will be to detract from the image. As a rule of thumb, the camera-to-subject distance should be no greater than a quarter of the visibility. A wider angle lens enables you to move closer and minimise the particle-laden water between camera and subject. A light mounted close to the camera will illuminate more of the particles in the water than a light held away from the camera. Besides giving a better modelling light to the subject, the light positioned further away illuminates fewer particles between camera and subject (*see* fig. 21).

Successful pictures can be taken using available light in the top 5 m of water. Light is progressively filtered out as you go deeper. Different colours are absorbed at different rates: first the reds turn black, then orange and yellow are filtered out. An underwater strobe or video lamp is needed to provide enough light to take the pictures *and* to restore the true colours. Film speeds of between ISO 50 and ISO 100 are ideal. Grainier fast films are not appropriate in strong sunlight near the surface or when using artificial light.

Taking pictures

Test the camera gear in a swimming pool before taking it into the sea. Avoid shooting haphazardly by having an idea of what you want to take before the dive. The most satisfying shots are usually clear and simple. Consider telling the full story of a dive. Begin with shots of the preparations, then the dive location, perhaps including the boat or beach. Take pictures of other divers kitting up then taking the plunge. Include a variety of subjects underwater, such as close-ups of fish or rock formations and your buddy exploring the sea bed.

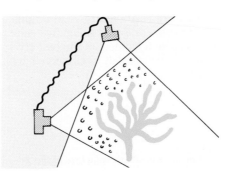

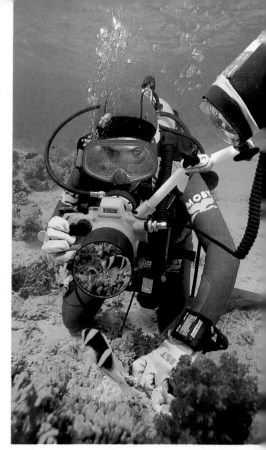

▲ *Fig. 21 A flashgun near the camera will illuminate suspended particles between the lens and the subject. Reduce this by positioning the flash away from the camera*

Where to dive

With 70% of the earth's surface covered with water, the potential for sport diving is tremendous. Anywhere with fewer than 45 m of water is fair game for the diver, depending on his experience and the conditions at the time. Begin near home, with day trips to the sea, lakes or rivers. Take your first diving holiday with a club or specialist dive tour operator, and learn from the way they handle the logistical arrangements. Qualified operators know the best dive locations and have already negotiated travel and accommodation costs.

By diving from an existing dive centre you have ready access to equipment hire, compressed air and, in many cases, dive boats. Ideally, take your own mask, snorkel, lifejacket, diving suit, accessories and possibly fins. If you take your own small cylinder on a plane, pack it empty with the valve open. If diving with new people, check their understanding of the hand signals and safety procedures before the dive. Agree which dive tables are to be used. Find out about local hazards or conditions that may affect diving.

Unless you have your own compressor you are restricted to destinations around the world that have dive centres. Fortunately, most of the best dive locations are already well served by dive centres.

You can dive almost anywhere in the ▶ world as long as you have access to a compressor to pump air into the diving cylinder

North America has an enormous variety of diving opportunities in the freshwater lakes of Wisconsin, New York State and Florida as well as in the Great Lakes. Many wrecks lie within easy reach off the east coast, especially between Charleston and Boston. Water around the Florida Keys is warm with good visibility and rich in marine life. Boats take divers to the best sites.

You can snorkel with dolphins at two or three locations in the Florida Keys. After a briefing session about how to behave in the water, you swim and duck dive with them in their enclosure. It is an enchanting experience, surpassed only by the thrill of swimming with wild dolphins in the open sea. The dolphins are regularly released, but keep returning for the food and, perhaps, the human contact, which they seem to enjoy.

The Gulf of California offers the possibility of diving with whales, huge manta rays and sea lions. The volcanoes of Hawaii have created breathtaking caves and drop-offs suitable for beach and boat dives.

The waters of the **Caribbean** are warm, the visibility is usually good, and marine life is abundant in places. Barbados is good for beach and boat diving. The west coast of Bonaire is lined with a spectacular coral reef, often accessible from the beach. The Cayman Islands has excellent dive facilities and superb beach and boat dive sites. Cozumel has good dive facilities and many impressive beach and boat dives. Cuba offers some very good boat dives to wrecks and coral drop-offs. Jamaica has a good variety of dives suitable for beginners and experienced divers. St Lucia is rich in sea life with many stunning dive sites. The US and British Virgin Islands are volcanic islands fringed with coral reefs which shelter an abundance of marine life in shallow water. The waters around Venezuela's Caribbean islands remain largely unexplored, though there is great potential.

The 700 islands of the **Bahamas** are washed by the warm water of the Gulf Stream. Many dive centres offer a range of diving experiences, including drift dives, wrecks, drop-offs and enchanting coral gardens.

Europe offers a variety of opportunities from the Norwegian fiords to the islands of the Mediterranean. Britain has a long history of diving and is well equipped with facilities, although the temperature of its waters seldom rise above 16°C (60°F) in summer. Cold water, variable visibility and testing currents help produce divers who are able to cope with some of the most adverse conditions. Numerous wrecks are scattered around the coast. The Azores (Portugal) are good for boat dives to caves and canyons. The Canary Islands (Spain) have several dive centres, the most popular of which are on the volcanic island of Lanzarote. Madeira (Portugal) has a number of caves and drop-offs and rich marine life. Norway's fiords offer spectacular clear water but little marine life.

The Mediterranean is generally warm, though the water is polluted in places and over-fished. Crete has some good archaeological dives. Corfu has steep drop-offs and caves reached by boat. Cyprus offers a range of excellent dive sites supported by very good facilities. France has many good sites especially along the south coast, with an

The air and water temperature is warm all year. Marine life is abundant and visibility is usually excellent. The most popular dive sites are located along the east coast of the Sinai Desert between Eilat and Ras Muhammed, and along the coast of mainland Egypt near Hurghada and Safaga.

The **Indian Ocean** is generally warm with abundant sea life. Kenya's east coast has an underwater reserve rich in marine life. The Maldives comprise a string of coral atolls with fringing reefs. Dive facilities are good. Mauritius is volcanic with a barrier reef which protects the beaches from currents and sharks. The sheltered inside of the reef is ideal for novice divers. The Seychelles offer extensive coral reefs and dramatic drop-offs, with beach and boat diving for beginners and experienced divers. Sri Lanka has a rich fringing coral reef, often accessible from the beach.

The **Far East** offers the most dramatic war wrecks. Malaysia and Sulawesi have recently developed good dive operations to explore excellent dive sites. Palau has some dive facilities and lots of exotic corals. The Philippines

excellent network of facilities. Italy has the facilities but the waters are overfished. Malta and Gozo has some of the best diving in the Mediterranean suitable for both novice and experienced divers. Spain offers good opportunities along the Costa Brava with caverns, tunnels and plenty of marine life.

The **Red Sea** is perhaps the most ideal dive location in the world. Facilities are excellent, with several dive boats, dive centres and dive schools.

has a few dive centres with boats to take you to some of the numerous, often unexplored coral gardens. Truk Lagoon in Micronesia is the best known site of hundreds of wrecks of Japanese planes and ships sunk during World War II. The waters around Papua New Guinea are also littered with World War II wrecks as well as diverse and undamaged coral reefs, served by live-aboard boats and land-based dive operations.

Australia's gem is the Great Barrier Reef stretching 2,000 km parallel to the north-east coast. It offers both tame dives on shallow reefs and spectacular dives on the coral drop-offs of the Outer Reef. Many centres cater for all standards, with beach dives and live-aboard boats. In South Australia, Kangaroo Island offers the chance to dive with seals and on wrecks. Tasmania and the Bass Strait island have good wreck dives.

New Zealand has a number of dive operations, especially on the North Island in the Bay of Islands. Nearby, the Poor Knights islands feature dramatic underwater scenery, good visibility and abundant marine life.

Divers' code
of conduct

- Leave a good impression by being considerate.
- Avoid antisocial behaviour.
- Don't obstruct roads/public places.
- Locate the compressor away from people who may be disturbed by the noise.
- Don't spread gear or litter around the beach or jetty.
- Adhere to local rules and regulations, and obey instructions given by local officials.
- Keep away from fishermen's nets, pots or buoys unless you have the opportunity to help.
- Fly the 'A' flag.
- Don't damage the marine environment.
- Don't use a speargun with scuba gear.
- Don't take fish, lobster, etc. smaller than the permitted size.
- Don't remove anything from wrecks or archaeological sites without permission.

Useful addresses

British Sub-Aqua Club (BSAC)
Telford's Quay
Ellesmere Port
South Wirral
Cheshire L65 4FY

Confédération Mondiale des Activités Subaquatiques (CMAS)
Siete Administratif
Viale Tiziano 74
00196 Rome
Italy

National Association of Underwater Instructors (NAUI)
PO Box 14650
Montclair
California 91763-1150
USA

Professional Association of Diving Instructors (PADI)
1251 East Dyer Road
#100
Santa Ana
California 92705-5605
USA

Scuba Schools International (SSI)
2619 Canton Court
Fort Collins
Colorado 80525
USA

Sub-Aqua Association (SAA)
Bryslan House
Upper Street
Fleet
Hampshire GU13 9PE

Index